LIVING
ZERO WASTE

BY ROBIN TWIDDY

One SMALL STEP
for kids

One giant leap
towards SAVING
the WORLD!

SMALL
STEPS
REVOLUTIONARIES

BookLife
PUBLISHING

©2021
BookLife Publishing Ltd.
King's Lynn
Norfolk, PE30 4LS

All rights reserved.
Printed in Malta.

A catalogue record for
this book is available from
the British Library.

ISBN: 978-1-83927-850-1

Written by:
Robin Twiddy

Edited by:
Madeline Tyler

Designed by:
Drue Rintoul

PHOTO CREDITS

Images are courtesy of Shutterstock.com. With thanks to Getty Images, Thinkstock Photo and iStockphoto.
4&5 – sirikorn thamniyom, Hung Chung Chih, Kev Gregory, VanderWolf Images, Lesterman, Belovodchenko
Anton, Mr.anaked, Krakenimages.com, Asier Romero, Krakenimages.com, Prostock-studio, Asier Romero.
6&7 – Semiletava Hanna. 8&9 – sirikorn thamniyom, ronstik, LightField Studios, Gwoeii, Toa55, DeawSS,
Ivanenko.PRO. 10&11 – sirikorn thamniyom, RONEDYA, MOHAMED ABDULRAHEEM, chaiyapruek youprasert,
Focus_Vector, Lyudmyla Kharlamova, Banana Walking, Eny Setiyowati, aririnstory. 12&13 – sirikorn thamniyom,
Friends Stock, vilax, SVStudio, Sellwell. 14&15 – Volurol, Africa Studio, Zmiter, K-D-uk, VectorShow, MaryValery,
happymay. 16&17 – dave_liza, ITTIGallery, Asier Romero, sirikorn thamniyom, Imfoto, ajt. 18&19 – nito, sirikorn
thamniyom, AshTproductions, Merrimon Crawford, Ratchanee Sawasdijira, Asier Romero. 20&21 – sirikorn
thamniyom. 22&23 – Max Topchii, Asier Romero, Ruslan Kudrin, Top Photo Engineer, Lalandrew, Krakenimages.
com, alexandre zveiger. 24&25 – sirikorn thamniyom, Krakenimages.com, Prostock-studio, vlastas, aoy jira,
loocmill, vladfromstock, Suti Stock Photo, Zurijeta, Cozine. 26&27 – sirikorn thamniyom, Monkey Business
Images. 28&29 – Dmytro Zinkevych, rangizzz. 30 – Dan Kosmayer, vi73, sirikorn thamniyom.

CONTENTS

Words that look like this are explained in the glossary on page 31.

You can (help) Save the World

The world is in trouble and it needs your help! It needs everyone's help. No one can save the world on their own, but together we can make a change. Our planet is facing many challenges, and lots of these are because of humans. The climate crisis is a big problem. We can see how humans have made it worse by looking at changes in the weather, the oceans and the air we breathe.

WEARING MASKS

AAAAAAAA AAAAARRR RGHHH!

TRAFFIC FUMES FILL THE AIR!

PLASTIC FILLS THE OCEANS!

FACTORIES CHOKE THE SKY!

SLUDGE FROM FACTORIES POURS INTO THE OCEAN!

WILDLIFE IS HURT

ROBIN TWIDDY PRESENTS:

THE SMALL STEPS REVOLUTIONARIES

Watch with amazement as the Small Steps Revolutionaries save the world one small step at a time!

Formed to save the world, the Small Steps Revolution gains new members every day!

Featuring Grant – the Zero Waste revolutionary!

These are the Small Steps Revolutionaries. They are changing the world one step at a time. Whether it's being energy efficient or learning how to <u>compost</u>, eating locally or living zero waste, recycling or using water wisely, no problem is too big or too small for this band of heroes. By the time you finish this book you too will be a member of the Small Steps Revolution. Strap in, recruit – it's time to save the world!

Grow Your Knowledge

The first step to becoming a **Small Steps Revolutionary** is growing your knowledge. This means learning as much as you can about the change you want to see. There are lots of ways to grow your knowledge. Here are some places to get started.

Visit the library — ask the librarian to help you find books about the <u>environment</u>.

Learn from others — do you know anyone who is already living zero waste? Ask them about it.

"Knowledge is power — arm yourself!"

Bertrand Russell was a British <u>philosopher</u> who spent his life thinking about how we can live a good life.

"The good life is one inspired by love and guided by knowledge." — Bertrand Russell

Geeta Iyengar was a yoga teacher in India. She did lots of good work for women in yoga.

"Knowledge has a beginning but no end." — Geeta Iyengar

Research online — there are lots of great websites about living zero waste.

"Those who do not learn from history are doomed to repeat it!"

Check your local council's website to find out about recycling in your area.

Use an online carbon dioxide (CO_2) calculator to find out what your carbon footprint is. (Find out more about your carbon footprint on page 9.)

SMALL STEP: GROW YOUR KNOWLEDGE!

Knowledge is important but make sure that the information you look at is accurate. A good way to do that is to see who else agrees, writes or talks about the same information. Has it come from a reliable place or person?

Live Like There Is a Tomorrow

Grant is a **Small Steps Revolutionary**. Being a Small Steps Revolutionary means making small changes in your own life to help make a _global_ change and inspire others to do the same.

"There is already too much waste in the world and I don't want to add to it. That is why I joined the **SMALL STEPS REVOLUTION!**"

"I am living zero waste, or at least I am trying to. Living zero waste means that you are careful not to make any waste that will end up going to _landfill_. It isn't easy living zero waste, so it is best to start with some **Small Steps**. I will help you get started."

THE SCOURGE OF GREENHOUSE GASES

Carbon Footprint

We all have a carbon footprint – this is the amount of carbon dioxide (CO_2) that we add to the environment through the things we do, buy and throw away. Living zero waste will help you to lower your carbon footprint.

Recruit an adult to help you calculate your carbon footprint online. Doing this will help you to understand how much CO_2 is produced by all the little things we do each day.

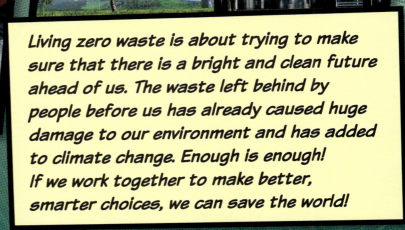

SMALL STEP: MEASURE YOUR CARBON FOOTPRINT

Living zero waste is about trying to make sure that there is a bright and clean future ahead of us. The waste left behind by people before us has already caused huge damage to our environment and has added to climate change. Enough is enough! If we work together to make better, smarter choices, we can save the world!

World of Waste

People waste more than they think they do. It is easy to waste. We don't often think about what happens to the things we put into the bin, but we should.

Lots of our waste goes to landfill. It breaks down slowly and releases methane and CO_2 into the atmosphere. Methane and CO_2 are greenhouse gases, which means they affect the climate crisis.

Sometimes waste is incinerated. Waste sent to incinerators is burned to make power. This is better than sending waste to landfill, but it still releases CO_2.

Some waste can end up <u>polluting</u> water and destroying animals' homes.

YOU CAN'T RECYCLE EVERYTHING

We should try to recycle as much as we can but there is some waste that is either hard to recycle or cannot be recycled, such as:

Crisp packets are really difficult to recycle and you can't put them in your normal recycling bin. There are some recycling companies that take crisps – see if you can find one near you.

Sticky notes cannot be recycled because of the glue on them that makes them sticky.

Kitchen roll can't be recycled even though normal paper can. Kitchen roll is often made from already recycled paper and could be covered in food waste.

Shredded or small paper cause the recycling machines to become clogged, so most recycling plants will not take it. Compost instead of recycling.

Cotton wool is made from cotton. If it has not been used to remove make-up it can be composted.

Tissues and wipes cannot be recycled even though they are made from paper. They can be composted, though.

We need to be sure that what we put in our recycling bins can actually be recycled. But don't worry, even if your local recycling service can't recycle something there might be another way to get rid of that waste in an environmentally friendly way.

SMALL STEP: LEARN WHAT CAN AND CANNOT BE RECYCLED IN YOUR AREA

How Much Waste?

If you want to start making **Small Steps** towards living zero waste, you will need to find out how much waste you are making each week.

Waste can be sorted into five <u>categories</u> – you are going to need a separate container for each of these:

PLASTIC AND RUBBER

GLASS

WASTE FOR COMPOSTING

PAPER AND CARDBOARD

<u>TOXIC</u> WASTE

Label your five containers and make sure that everyone in your house puts their waste into the right containers. After a week, you should be able to see how much waste your house is making.

Glass

Paper and cardboard

Toxic waste

Plastic and rubber

Waste for composting

NOW WHAT?

Remember, knowledge is power. Learning about what waste you make each week will help you plan your next step. Look at the waste you have collected at the end of each day, and make sure you look at the waste that can't be recycled. Look for items that there is a lot of and write down what they are.

IT'S A DIRTY JOB BUT SOMEONE'S GOT TO DO IT!

If you are sorting through your waste at the end of the day, make sure that you are wearing gloves and recruit an adult to help you. Waste can be dirty or sharp, so be careful.

**SMALL STEP:
CALCULATE YOUR
WASTE**

Buy Less and Buy Smart

Living zero waste isn't just about being smart with the waste you make; it is also about stopping some of that waste before you make it. What does that mean? It means being smart about what you buy.

Use what you know from looking at your rubbish to work out how you are most wasteful.

Is there anything that you could give up to cut down on your waste?

Were there a lot of crisp packets?

You don't have to give up crisps completely. You could take a small step to reduce your waste. Instead of eating crisps every day, maybe you could try another snack instead.

Are there things you could snack on that would make less waste, or come in recyclable or biodegradable packaging? Or better yet, no packaging at all? Crunchy carrot sticks make a great snack. Fruit is another good healthy alternative to other snacks and comes with no, or very little, packaging.

WAYS TO MAKE YOUR SHOPPING ONE STEP CLOSER TO ZERO WASTE

Bring a reusable bag
By bringing bags with you, you can avoid having to buy extra bags.

Choose to buy things with less plastic packaging or without any packaging at all
The less packaging you buy, the less you will end up throwing away.

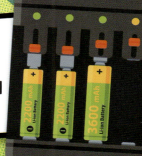

Buy in bulk
Things that you use a lot of or can be kept for a long time should be bought in bulk. This means buying a lot at the same time. Buying in bulk usually means there is less packaging.

Avoid single-use products
Try to buy things that can be used more than once. Using sandwich boxes instead of sandwich bags and rechargeable batteries instead of single-use batteries can help you to reduce your waste.

Buy only what you need
Try to make sure that you don't buy more than you need of things that will spoil. A lot of organic waste comes from food that goes off before we get to eat it.

SMALL STEP: THINK ABOUT WHAT YOU BUY, HOW MUCH AND WHETHER YOU NEED IT

Don't Bin It

Taking Small Steps towards living zero waste means sending less waste to landfill, but how do we do this? Morrison is an expert in recycling and upcycling.

You have heard about recycling and upcycling, but what do these words actually mean?

RECYCLING

When something is recycled, it is broken down, taken apart or melted to make something new. When something is made from recycled materials, it may not be as good or as strong as the things it used to be. This doesn't mean that recycled things are bad, though.

UPCYCLING

Upcycling is when something that is old or broken is used in a new way or made into something new. When something is upcycled, the new thing may still look like the old thing because it hasn't been broken down or melted. Upcycling means you can make new, working things out of old, broken things.

Food Waste

Food waste is a big problem. Food that gets put into our general waste bins gets buried at landfill sites. Organic waste, such as food, cannot break down properly in landfills. When we waste food, we are not just wasting food – we are wasting all of the energy used to grow and move that food. It is thought that about one-third of the food grown for humans is wasted.

That is way too much waste, but don't worry, there are some **Small Steps** we can take to make a difference.

LEFTOVERS

It is important to make sure that we aren't throwing away food for no reason. Here are some things that you can do to reduce your food waste.

Buy what you need – a lot of food waste is food that spoils before it even reaches our plates. If you can, it is better to buy less food but more often.

Save your leftovers – leftovers can make a great meal the next day and cut down on waste.

Compost your food waste – if you can't save your leftovers for another meal, don't put them in the bin. Organic waste such as food should be composted.

Did I hear the word composting? Now you're in my territory.

Composting is the best way to get rid of your food waste and it is really good for your garden too. But don't worry if you don't have a garden or the space to compost – lots of communities have food bins. The waste collected in these is taken away to be composted elsewhere.

If you want to learn more about composting and using your waste in the garden, check out my book, Composting and Gardening.

SMALL STEPS:
- COMPOST YOUR FOOD WASTE
- SAVE YOUR LEFTOVERS
- BUY WHAT YOU NEED ONLINE

Small Steps Today

The Small Steps Revolution is all about making small, sustainable changes. When you make a change to your everyday life it can be hard to keep to it, but stick with it and those changes will become normal to you. The trick is not to try and make too many changes at once.

It can get a little overwhelming if you try to do it all at once.

MAKING A **NEW** NORMAL

Sometimes it is hard to make a positive change that will bring you closer to living zero waste because no one else you know is doing it. Just because something is normal and everyone does it that way, it doesn't mean that it is right. Being a Small Steps Revolutionary means making your own normal!

I make my own normal!

Here are some Small Steps you can take today to move towards living zero waste.

Carry a reusable water bottle – you'll never have to buy plastic bottles again!

Carry a hanky – cut down on tissues by using a hanky for small sniffles.

Use bars of soap instead of bottled soap – cut out that plastic bottle!

Buy second-hand where you can – cut out that nasty packaging.

Borrow and lend things with your friends instead of buying them.

Learn to sew – with this skill you will be able to fix your own clothes or upcycle old material into new things.

Use pencils or refillable pens instead of single-use biros.

Bring your own bag – always carry a reusable bag. Why not have one that is your style!

Use less – it is easy to overuse things such as toothpaste and shampoo. If you are careful to use only what you need, you will replace them less often.

Making Better Choices

BAKE YOUR OWN!

DO YOU LIKE SANDWICHES? YOU DO?
DO YOU BUY BREAD FROM THE SHOPS? YOU DO?

Then I bet you end up with some nasty plastic packaging when the bread has all gone!
Well not anymore, thanks to home baking!

Side effects of home baking include: a sense of accomplishment, a healthier environment, less waste and nice bread.

Homemade Fashion

Are your clothes getting old?
Holes in your jeans?
T-shirts too small?

Don't throw them in the bin!!!!!

Be Like Morrison and upcycle your fashion! Cut up old t-shirts and shirts to make cool patches to fix your clothes.
Save the environment and look cool doing it!

Be Cool, Don't be a Plastic Fool

We all get thirsty when we are playing with our friends. Don't be like Percy Polluter who buys expensive bottled water to bring to the playing field. Be like Cathy! She carries a reusable metal water bottle that keeps her tap water cool while she stays even cooler.

REUSABLE!

DORK

KEEPS IT COOL!

ZERO WASTE!

ENVIRONMENTALLY FRIENDLY!

THE SMALL STEPS REVOLUTION NEEDS YOU!

CALLING ALL KIDS. IT IS TIME TO MAKE A DIFFERENCE. DO YOU HAVE WHAT IT TAKES TO JOIN THE SMALL STEPS REVOLUTION? YOU *CAN* MAKE A DIFFERENCE! TO BECOME A MEMBER, SIMPLY TAKE ONE OF THE SMALL STEPS IN THIS BOOK, TAKE SOME PICTURES AND SHARE THEM WITH THE HASHTAG #SMALLSTEPSREVOLUTION

AMAZING Blank Pages

ARE YOU TIRED OF RUNNING OUT OF DRAWING PAPER? WITH OUR NEW FLIPPING TECHNIQUE, TURN OLD USED PAPER INTO NEW BLANK PAPER! THE TECHNIQUE IS SIMPLE — WHEN YOU HAVE FINISHED WRITING OR DRAWING ON A PIECE OF PAPER, TURN IT OVER!!!!

HALF YOUR PAPER USAGE TODAY!

BEFORE

TEST A+

AFTER

All New Card—Maker

Don't buy a card, make a card. Use your imagination to create something special and unique.

"I LOVE MY HOMEMADE CARD!"

"WOW, YOU MADE THIS YOURSELF?"

Card Maker

"IT REALLY SHOWS THAT YOU CARE!"

Results include little to no waste, a thoughtful gift, gratitude and a Small Step towards saving the world.

23

Invisible Waste

We have looked at a lot of ways that you can reduce or completely get rid of the waste in your life, but did you realise that we make waste when we aren't wise with our power and water? When we eat crisps, we're left with the empty packet, and when we buy new toys, we may throw away the plastic packaging. It's harder to see the waste we make from using power and water.

My friends Ron and Kim are experts at being wise with power and water.

Hi, I am Kim. I am an expert on being **Energy Efficient**.

Yo, I'm Ron. I am an expert on being **Wise with Water**. Grant is right, when we use water and power, waste is being made in power plants and water is being taken from natural areas. We need to make sure that we are being wise with what we use.

To be **Energy Efficient** you need to think about the power you use and the ways you can save energy. Here are a few tips...

Switch off lights when you leave a room.

Open the curtains in the day instead of turning on the lights.

Don't use standby mode – switch it off at the wall.

That is some great advice, Kim. To be **Wise with Water** you need to think in a similar way. Here are some tips that will help you...

Take showers instead of baths – they use less water.

Don't leave the tap running when you brush your teeth.

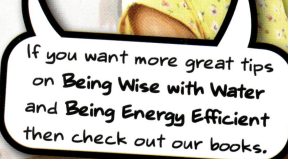

If you want more great tips on **Being Wise with Water** and **Being Energy Efficient** then check out our books.

Use cups of water that you aren't going to drink to water plants or give to pets.

Becoming a Champion of Change

Being a Small Steps Revolutionary is more than just taking Small Steps yourself – it also means being a champion for change. We can do this by showing others the steps we are taking and sharing our passion for living zero waste.

RAISING AWARENESS

There are lots of ways that you can raise awareness as a Small Steps Revolutionary. Some revolutionaries use social media to share their message. Recruit an adult to help you manage an account. Remember not to use social media without an adult you trust.

If you are artistic or creative, you could decorate your bag or make a t-shirt with messages that promote living zero waste.

LIVING ZERO WASTE.

Look for places that you can make a change. Are there any Small Steps that could help your school to make less waste? Talk to a teacher and see if you can help them to make a change.

Be the change you want to see.

I got my school to have more recycling bins.

Small Steps Revolutionaries are proud to make a change!

Share your successes with the hashtag #smallstepsrevolution

Remember, some people might not have met anyone making the changes you are making, so be nice when you talk about living zero waste. People are more likely to try to make a change themselves if you are helpful instead of being mean to them – this is the Small Steps way!

SMALL STEP: UPCYCLE AND RECYCLE

Ethical Living

Living zero waste is only one part of the Small Steps Revolution, so what does it mean to be a Small Steps Revolutionary? It means living ethically – living the best life you can. To live ethically you need to think about the effect your actions have on the world around you.

Making the change to living zero waste is not easy and won't happen overnight. Remember the golden rule: Small Steps Lead to Big Change. Focus on making small changes that you can keep to every day; every small step will take you closer to living zero waste.

THE FIVE Rs

REFUSE – BEFORE YOU BUY SOMETHING, THINK HARD ABOUT WHETHER YOU NEED IT OR NOT. IF YOU DON'T, THEN REFUSE TO BUY OR USE IT.

REDUCE – SOME THINGS YOU WILL NOT BE ABLE TO REFUSE, BUT YOU CAN USE LESS. THIS WILL MEAN YOU CREATE LESS WASTE.

REUSE – BEFORE YOU THROW SOMETHING AWAY, THINK ABOUT WHETHER THAT THING CAN BE USED AGAIN. ONLY REPLACE SOMETHING IF IT CAN'T BE USED AGAIN.

REPURPOSE – THIS IS ANOTHER WAY OF SAYING UPCYCLE. IF YOU CAN, FIND A NEW WAY TO USE SOMETHING INSTEAD OF THROWING IT AWAY.

RECYCLE – IF YOU CAN'T DO ANY OF THESE THINGS THEN YOU SHOULD TRY TO RECYCLE. MAKE SURE THAT WHAT YOU PUT INTO YOUR RECYCLING BIN CAN BE RECYCLED BY YOUR LOCAL RECYCLING CENTRE.

Manifesto

- GROW YOUR KNOWLEDGE
- MEASURE YOUR CARBON FOOTPRINT
- LEARN WHAT CAN AND CANNOT BE RECYCLED IN YOUR AREA
- CALCULATE YOUR WASTE
- THINK ABOUT WHAT YOU BUY, HOW AND WHETHER YOU NEED IT
- COMPOST YOUR FOOD
- SAVE YOUR LEFTOVERS
- BUY ONLY WHAT YOU NEED
- RECYCLE
- UPCYCLE

You are now a full member of the **Small Steps Revolution**. Keep on taking small, sustainable steps, spreading the word and inspiring others to do the same. Together we can and will **Save the World**.

Glossary

ACCOMPLISHMENT   having achieved or done something well

BIODEGRADABLE   to break down due to living things such as bacteria

CALCULATE   to work out something

CARBON DIOXIDE   a natural colourless gas found in air

CATEGORIES   separate groups or sections of something

CLIMATE CRISIS   serious problems being caused by changes to the world's weather, caused by humans and the release of greenhouse gases into the environment

COMPOST   to let natural things rot together in a way that makes nutrients that are good for soil

ENVIRONMENT   all the things that make up the natural world

GLOBAL   to do with the whole world

LANDFILL   where waste is buried

ORGANIC WASTE   a type of waste that is made up of natural things such as food

PHILOSOPHER   a person who studies the nature of reality and existence

POLLUTING   adding something poisonous and harmful to the environment

RECRUIT   to bring a member into a group

RELIABLE   can be trusted

SINGLE-USE PRODUCTS   things that can be bought that are meant to be used once and thrown away

SPOIL   to go off, or be ruined

TOXIC   poisonous, harmful

UNIQUE   special or unusual, unlike any other

Index